Golden Anniversary Acquisitions

SEPTEMBER 10 THROUGH OCTOBER 16

This exhibition celebrates the *raison d'être* of an art museum: the collection, presentation, and display of important, rare, and beautiful works of art. History and our tradition confirm the power of these works to move and delight those who contemplate them. Given the ability and the opportunity, no art museum can ignore the vitality inherent in an excellent permanent collection. Not only do these works mean many things to many persons but the individual finds in them constantly changing and ever renewed meanings on various levels. The masterpieces of the great museums of the world are visited and revisited not merely for their monetary value or their status-granting capacities, but essentially for their constant capacity for initial and renewed delight. If H. L. Mencken found no painting worthy of more than a few seconds' attention, it was because the word was *his* obsession. The literary works of painters are seldom, if ever, worth a tithe of their pictorial essays. Heine's "I am a picture; do not ask me to speak," goes to the heart of the matter.

Our Museum has been fortunate from the beginning in the visible determination of its Trustees, donors, and staff to accumulate artistic wealth. We would be less than candid if we did not admit our desire to provide a particularly rewarding display of acquisitions for this Year in Review on our Golden Anniversary. In addition to our regular major institutional sources of purchase income—the J. H. Wade, John L. Severance, Mr. and Mrs. William H. Marlatt, and Leonard C. Hanna Jr. Bequest Funds—The John Huntington Art and Polytechnic Trust has most generously provided additional means to achieve the results we now present. Without the encouragement of the Trustees and the researchers of the curatorial staff little could have been accomplished.

The time span and geographic areas available to the general art museum are, to say the least, extensive. We are not committed to any one medium, style, country, or period. The artistic accomplishment of man is our charge, and this exhibition, representing but slightly more than a year of activity, reveals the extent of our responsibilities. This may sound as if there were a program or schedule for accessions. While there is planning—the strengthening of strengths, the solid replacement of voids, the insistence on high quality and excellent condition—there must also be improvisation. Who could have planned for, or predicted, the sudden wealth of Spanish painting available to us? Like a military campaigner, one begins with strategy, continues with tactics, and ends with responses to local situations. The day is long past when one could determine to have, for example, a really fine collection of Italian High Renaissance painting or of Medieval sculpture. But easy despair finds solace in the still continuing, if irregular, appearance of riches on the art markets of the world. The years go by and the once apparently isolated works of art acquired assume their rightful places beside their peers; the collections grow in richness and provide understanding. What more satisfying and encouraging reward can there be than the opportunity to contemplate the visual achievements of man as artist, wherever their origin or by whomever they may be?

Sherman E. Lee, Director

125 *Beaker,* gold, repoussé and engraved, Northwestern Iran, ca.1000 B.C.

ABOVE LEFT
6 *Octodrachnum*,
gold, Egypt, 261 B.C.

ABOVE
3 *Cameo Representing Artemis,*
opaque glass, Roman,
early 1st century A.D. (?)

129 *Rhyton: The Angel Dravspa,*
silver, repoussé and engraved,
partially gilded, Iran (?),
Sasanian Period, 4th–5th century

2 *Cameo of Zeus and Hera*
Seated Flanked by an Eros
and Their Daughter Hebe,
South Italy, 1st century B.C.

186

127 *Ewer,* silver,
Iran, Sasanian Period

OPPOSITE
130 *Textile Fragment* (detail),
silk, Iran, Buyid Period,
10th–11th century

30 *Intaglio,* rock crystal with gilt-silver frame, Early Christian, 4th century

51 *Spoon,* silver, silver gilt, and niello, Early Christian, 4th century

OPPOSITE

126 *Beaker,* gold, Iran, Buyid Period, 985–998

This gold ewer is inscribed with the name of Samsam al-Dawla, an emir of the Buyid dynasty, who ruled over Iraq and Iran between A.D. 985 and 998. The ewer is said to have been found together with a series of rich silks in tombs in the necropolis at Raiy, the medieval capital of Iran (not far from present-day Teheran). There is no assurance that the ewer was actually found in the tomb of Samsam al-Dawla, but that it was is strongly suggested by the fact that among the silks recovered from this site there is one with the inscribed date, 338 H./A.D. 998, which might well have been used for his burial in that year. This silk is also in the Museum's collection (published, February 1956 *Bulletin*); hence, it is particularly fitting that the gold ewer should at last be reunited with it. The ewer, which was formed by hammering up from a single sheet of gold, was decorated by the repoussé technique (hammering out from within) and engraving. D.G.S.

36 *Monogram of Christ (Chrismon),* gold with garnets, Byzantium, Syria, 6th–7th century

Carved from blocks of the same white-grained, well-crystallized marble, these eleven sculptures are thought to have come from the same source in the Eastern Mediterranean. Two natural patinas in a fairly orderly pattern over each piece indicate that they were partially buried together over a long period. The three pairs of busts (only one pair illustrated) follow in the Mediterranean tradition of late Roman official portraiture. The five symbolic figures have a strongly Hellenistic flavor, with their motifs of river god, sea monster, and Serapis and Alexander head types. Stylistic analogies and details of coiffure suggest that the group dates from the late third century. It is perfectly plausible that the two "modes" were produced not only at the same time but in the same workshop; the artists must simply have used the familiar tradition best suited for each type of subject. No other free-standing pairs of busts are known, although they must have existed in quantity, judging from the paired relief busts on Early Christian sarcophagi. The symbolic figures are either rare or unique as free-standing subjects to be viewed from three sides. The *Good Shepherd* is

43 *Jonah Swallowed by the Whale*

44 *Jonah under the Gourd Vine*

40 *Portrait Bust of a Woman*

known in only about fifteen marble examples, from either the Greek Mediterranean or Rome in the Latin West, of which number this is the best preserved. The free-standing *Orant Figure* and *Jonah under the Gourd Vine* are unique, and, except for one marble group found at Tarsus in 1876, so are the Jonahs swallowed and cast up. The symbolic references to resurrection, life after death, and salvation are clearly Christian. If the busts are different members of one family, and if all were intended as one ensemble, we may have a uniquely preserved program for the deluxe funerary *cubiculum* of an important Christian family. Analogies exist in Early Christian sarcophagi, catacomb paintings, and possibly also mosaics. Another possibility is that these are the remains of a sculptor's studio meant to be divided. The portraits, if depicting one couple in series, may have been intended as gifts or commemorations like consular diptychs. The symbolic sculptures might have been for some other purpose, perhaps a fountain. The localization of the entire group in a once-great Hellenistic center, possibly Antioch, in the Eastern Mediterranean is clear from the evidence of the marble, the motifs, and details of costume and style. The sculptural quality, rare in preserved Early Christian art, is evident in the bold, writing movement of the whale episodes and the idyllic repose of *Jonah under the Gourd Vine*. The *Good Shepherd* and *Orant Figure* have an unusual nobility and monumentality—the latter's evocative dignity and simplicity make it one of the most moving depictions of a figure in prayer in the entire history of art. w.d.w.

41 *The Good Shepherd*

45 *Orant Figure (Jonah?)*

48 *Portrait Bust of a Man*

53 *Two Kneeling Carthusian Monks,* marble, France, end of 14th century

Two kneeling monks, hands in an attitude of prayer, look upward to some now-lost object of veneration. They represent monks of the Carthusian order, for they are shown wearing the *scapulaire* of that order. In their lyricism, as in the soft modeling of draperies, they reflect the elegant art of Paris in the last quarter of the fourteenth century. They are the only known existing relief sculptures of this subject from this century or the following one and they are extremely rare as kneeling figures in prayer. As proposed by Germain Seligman, there is a good possibility that they were formerly part of the sculptural decoration of the Chartreuse de Paris, now completely destroyed, but recorded in descriptions and old engravings. The original context of these two relief sculptures may have been a devotional one. w.d.w.

194

55 Jean de Beaumetz, *The Calvary with a Carthusian Monk,* oak panel

56 Berlinghiero, *The Madonna and Child with Saints,* triptych, poplar panels

The earliest picture of the Italian school to enter the painting collection of the Museum is this triptych by Berlinghiero, formerly in the distinguished collection of Adolphe Stoclet, Brussels. The eldest of a family of Lucchese painters, Berlinghiero is known definitely by a single signed work, a *Crucifix* in the Pinacoteca, Lucca, probably painted between 1210 and 1220. The present triptych, in superlative condition, bears every mark of association with the original master, in minutest detail of painting—eyes, features, fingers—and is especially characteristic in the figures of the Madonna and Child. While in the Stoclet Collection this tabernacle was first recognized as in the style of Berlinghiero by the late Richard Offner, and it was subsequently published by E. B. Garrison as the work of an advanced follower of the master. Berlinghiero introduced to Lucca a Byzantine style of painting which dominated that school during the first three quarters of the thirteenth century and strongly influenced painting in Pisa and Florence as well. H.S.F.

196

42 *Jonah Cast Up,* marble, Eastern Mediterranean, late 3rd century

60 Giovanni di Paolo, *St. Catherine of Siena and the Beggar* (above) , and *St. Catherine of Siena Invested with the Dominican Habit by SS. Dominic, Augustine, and Francis* (opposite) , panels

200

91 Albrecht Dürer
St. Jerome in Penitence,
engraving

OPPOSITE
31 *Kneeling Prophet,*
gilt bronze,
Franco-Netherlands,
ca. 1400

This small gilt-bronze sculpture embodies a conception of an Old Testament prophet which is at once monumental, powerful, and subtle. The figure seems poised momentarily in action. With his lips parted and his head pulled forward, his beard is windblown away from the direction of his attentive gaze. The suspended movement of the figure was once further underscored by a curvilinear banderole which was formerly held in the *Prophet's* outstretched hands. Symbolically, this figure is an heir to a long tradition of representations of figures inspired by some outer force, the gift of prophecy or the Word. The Cleveland *Kneeling Prophet,* completely unknown until its recent discovery, was first connected by Herbert Bier with a similar *Kneeling Prophet* of the same dimensions, material, gilding, and style preserved in the Louvre since 1903, which has been generally related to the art of André Beauneveu of Valenciennes. However, both sculptures can be more closely compared with some of the sculptures carved by Claus Sluter at the Chartreuse de Champmol near Dijon for Philip the Bold, Duke of Burgundy. The two bronzes may have been part of a base for a cross or a support for a Virgin and Child group. W.D.W.

201

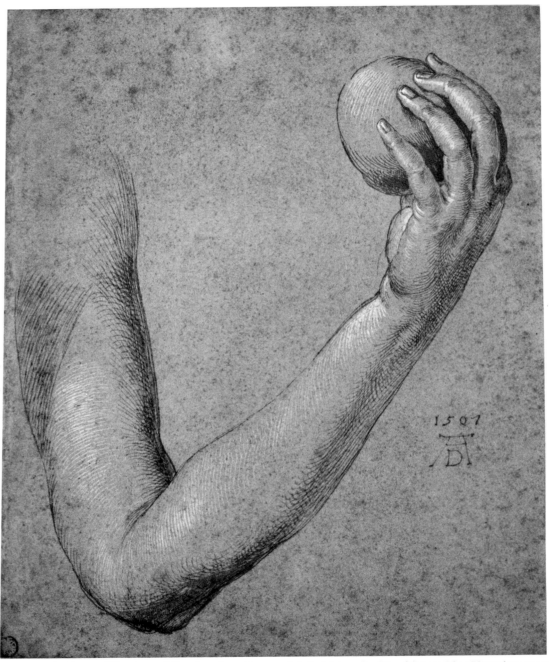

89 Albrecht Dürer, *The Arm of Eve,* brush and brown ink heightened with white on blue Venetian paper

87 Nikolaus Manuel Deutsch I,
The Fifth Foolish Virgin, woodcut

74 Domenico Beccafumi, *Page from a Sketch Book:*
The Head of a Woman (recto) , black chalk

OPPOSITE: In the early months of 1507 Dürer returned to Germany from Venice. In September of the same year he completed two large, nearly life-size panel paintings of *Adam* and *Eve,* now in the Prado Museum in Madrid. This drawing for the left arm of Eve, to actual size, is the only known study for either of the panels. It is drawn on blue Venetian paper—colored paper was not then made in Germany—with a brush and dark brown and white ink. The shadow that falls across the upper arm in the painting is already indicated in the drawing, which becomes fuller and more three-dimensional as the elbow, lower arm, and hand emerge sharply modelled in dark and light lines against the pale color of the paper. This strength of form combined with delicacy of touch superbly exemplifies Dürer's draftsmanship at the beginning of his mature, most richly productive period. *The Arm of Eve* is well documented in the principal literature and comes from a series of distinguished collections. It was only by incredible good fortune that this large, beautiful page was available to complement the excellent collection of Dürer's prints and add a third major Dürer drawing to the *Dead Christ* and *Ascension.* L.E.P. L.S.R.

81 Frans Crabbe, *Adoration of the Shepherds,* engraving

70 Hans Baldung (called Grien),
The Bewitched Groom, woodcut

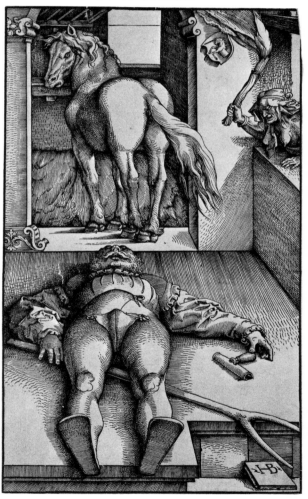

90 Albrecht Dürer, *The Holy Family
with Two Musician Angels,* woodcut

206

32 *Albarello: Putto Riding
a Wild Boar,* majolica,
Italy, Siena (?), ca.1510

112 Enea Vico, *Ewer Ornamented with Dolphins,* engraving

ROMÆ AB ANTIQVO REPERTVM   M. D. XXXXIII   E.V.

79 Luca Cambiaso, *Apollo Flaying Marsyas,*
pen and brown ink and ink wash

109 Philipp Uffenbach,
The Resurrection, etching

92 Anthony van Dyck,
The Lamentation,
black chalk, brush and ink,
heightened with white, on gray paper

111 Esias van de Velde,
*Hilly Landscape with
House beside a Stream,*
black chalk with
tan and gray washes

110 Adriaen van de Velde, *Seated Peasant Woman,* red chalk

88 Lambert Doomer, *View of Orleans on the Loire,*
pen and brown ink, brown and gray washes

67 Adriaen van de Velde,
*Landscape with
Sleeping Shepherdess,*
oil on wood

101 Prince Rupert
von der Pfalz,
Standard Bear
mezzotint

15 Johann
Andreas Thelot
Covered Cup
silver and
gilt silver

212

214

64 Bartolomé Estebán Murillo,
    Laban Searching for His Stolen Household Gods in Rachel's Tent, oil on canvas

59 Luca Giordano, *The Apparition of the Virgin to St. Francis of Assisi,* oil on canvas

61 Francisco José
de Goya y Lucientes,
*Portrait of the Infante
Don Luis de Borbón,*
oil on canvas

OPPOSITE: Painted by Goya during the years 1783–1784, this is one of the rare royal portraits to have left Spain. Goya's earliest commission under the patronage of the King came in 1776 to design cartoons for the royal tapestry manufactury. From then on he became increasingly employed by King Charles III and his Queen, Maria Luisa, repeatedly painting them and members of the royal family, among them the King's brother, the Infante Don Luis. Don Luis Antonio was the second son of Philip V and Isabel de Farnese; he was dedicated to the church, receiving a cardinal's hat at the age of eight. Though a scholar of considerable attainment, he gave up his ecclesiastical career in 1776 to marry a noble Aragonese, Doña Maria Teresa de Vallabriga, famous for her beauty and artistic interests. They lived in the country at Arenas de San Pedro, where Goya visited them in 1783. During several months there, he painted this picture, as well as that of Don Luis' wife and other members of the family. Goya became a devoted personal friend of the prince, with whom he hunted every day, and whose tastes he wholly shared. Such was the relationship which existed, that it was planned for future annual visits, only to be sadly broken shortly thereafter by the prince's death in 1785. This portrait of Don Luis is extraordinary, not alone for the beauty and brilliance of the painting, the sheen of silver and white, the rich blues and reds, the highly-keyed rendering of metals and jeweled ornaments, but most of all for the fact that Goya so achieved the likeness of his friend, whose kindness of soul, homely countenance, and penetrating blue eyes eclipse the richness of the fine detail throughout. The portrait thereby demonstrates not only Goya's genius as a painter, but the real and lasting personal relationship established between these two men. This portrait comes as an addition of first importance to the Museum's collection of paintings in this anniversary year. Representing the vigorous youthful accomplishment of Goya as a portraitist, it presents a noble contrast in treatment with Goya's *Don Juan Antonio Cuervo,* dated 1819, a portrait acquired in 1943 as the first purchase from the Marlatt Fund. These two paintings illustrate Goya's versatility as one of the world's most penetrating portraitists, and one who never ceased to increase in stature as he grew older. The *Cuervo* belongs as surely to the 19th century as does *Don Luis* to the 18th. H.S.F.

12 Antonio Lopez (probably) , *Chalice,* silver gilt

218

65 Jusepe de Ribera, *The Death of Adonis,* oil on canvas

16 *Baptism of Christ,* bronze, Italy, mid-17th century

66 Gabriel de Saint-Aubin, *Laban Cherchant ses Dieux,* oil on canvas

OPPOSITE 7 Circle of Georg Raphael Donner, *House Altarpiece,* gilded wood

The central relief of this altarpiece, a *Lamentation,* is based upon a composition by Georg Raphael Donner. The larger angels who flank the central relief also reveal Donner's influence. In contrast, however, are the other figures, the putti, and the God the Father, which show in their emotionally active draperies a stylistic tendency antithetical to that of Donner. The sculptor who carved this altarpiece must have both had intimate contact with Donner's works and experienced stylistic pressures from outside Donner's circle, perhaps from Prague or Bavaria. The style of the decorative elements of this altarpiece indicate that it must have been designed about 1740. Compartments around the perimeter of the altar contain relics of saints. The relic in the top central compartment is of St. Francis Xavier, indicating that this gilded wood altarpiece was made for a Jesuit. H.H.H.

This *Angel* was probably used as an element in the decoration of a small altarpiece. The flickering, almost faceted cutting of the surfaces intended to represent drapery is typical of the style of Ignaz Günther, the leading south German sculptor of the eighteenth century. The impressionistic handling of the drapery is accentuated by the loss of much of the original gessoed and painted surface of the figure, which was probably painted white. The *Angel* has also lost its wings, and several of its fingers have been replaced. These losses have not, however, seriously impaired the formal and expressive qualities of the figure as they were conceived by Günther. The work probably dates from about 1760. H.H.H.

9 Giovanni Battista Foggini, *David and Goliath,* terra cotta

13 Joseph-Charles Marin,
Bust of a Woman, terra cotta

14 Benjamin Pyne,
Monteith, silver

224

102 Gabriel de Saint-Aubin, *Fête in a Park with Costumed Dancers*,
ink, ink and water-color washes, over pencil indications

28 *Tureen in the Form of a Turtle,* faience, France, Strasbourg, 1750–1760

37 *Pot Pourri,* porcelain, France Vincennes, 1745–1750

8 Etienne-Maurice Falconet (after design by François Boucher), *The Fête at the Château,* porcelain

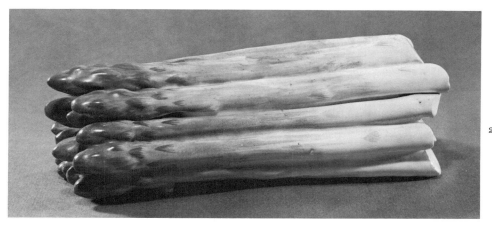

21 *Box in the Form of*
a Bunch of Asparagus,
faience, France,
Sceaux, ca.1765

19 *Cupid Carried by the Graces,* porcelain, France,
Sèvres, 1768 (after a design by François Boucher)

23 *Pair of Figures,*
faience, France, Strasbourg, 1745–1750

22 *Large Plate,*
faience, France, Nevers, ca.1700

26 *Plate with Two Crayfish,*
faience, France, Strasbourg, 1750–1760

27 *Round Box,* faience with burled wood casing,
France, Moustiers, style of Orleys Factory, ca.1750

25 *Plate Decorated with Playing Cards,* faience, France, Lille, ca.1750

20 *Bottle,* faience, France, Marseilles, Fauchier Factory, ca.1745

24 *Plate,* faience, France, St. Omer, ca.1760–1770

99 Samuel Palmer, *The Lonely Tower,* etching

54 Washington Allston, *Portrait of Samuel Williams,* oil on canvas

Le Campo Vaccino, près du haut du Colisée

95 Jean Baptiste Isabey, *Le Campo Vaccino,* from *Voyage en Italie en 1822,* bound album of 30 lithographs

OPPOSITE: This smallest and earliest of the four extant oil versions of the neo-classical subject, *Antiochus and Stratonice,* by Ingres, painted ca.1834, is in many respects the most subtle and most convincing, even though portions are left unfinished. (The first oil version done in 1825 is now unfortunately lost.) Besides a drawing for the first idea, now in the Louvre, there exist a considerable number of preparatory drawings, especially for the figure of Stratonice, one of these now in the collection of the Metropolitan Museum in New York. (A similarity of pose with this figure, which occupied Ingres so deeply in the versions of this subject, is to be found in the figure of the later portrait of Mme. d'Haussonville, now in the Frick Collection, New York.) Of the four oil versions, this earliest essay contains no elaborate Ionic canopy for the bed. The raised platform upon which Antiochus' couch rests projects in front of columns, seemingly the peristyle in the apartment, rather than supports for a baldachin for the bed as in the later examples. The light in all the versions falls most fully upon the figure of Stratonice; only in the Cleveland version does it reveal most clearly along the back wall of the apartment classical stories as if in fresco. One of these represents Theseus and the Minotaur, based on a drawing Ingres actually made after a fresco from Herculaneum, now in the Naples Museum. As Ingres elaborated the later and more grandiose versions of the *Antiochus and Stratonice,* he tended to emphasize the accessory detail and thereby obscured the very clearly defined neo-classical composition which is the feature of this particular example. Here the colors are rich and clear in the restrained manner of Ingres' best painting, and markedly distinct from the color schemes of romantic painting of the 1830's. Areas of the painting are not completely finished: parts of the wall paintings, Stratonice's robe, and the right arm of the doctor. Although the figure of Antiochus and the arms of Seleucus and Erasistratus are only lightly painted, the explicit gestures upon which Ingres concentrated so much thought tell the story vividly. H.S.F.

62 Jean Auguste Dominique Ingres, *Antiochus and Stratonice,* oil on canvas

63 Eastman Johnson, *Portrait of Mr. Gineo Scott,* oil on canvas

82 Nathaniel Currier, *American Farms Scenes, No. 4 (Winter),* lithograph colored by hand

86 Edgar Degas, *Esterel Village,* monotype

57 Eugène Louis Boudin, *Stormy Sky at Trouville,* oil on canvas

OPPOSITE: *Esterel Village* is the special and generous gift of The Print Club of Cleveland in celebration of the Museum's anniversary. It is an outstanding example of the high achievement of the acknowledged master of the monotype process. Degas was in large part responsible for the popularity of the monotype which continues to this day. He began with the simplest monotype technique, wiping an image in highlights from an evenly inked plate surface then printing it on moistened paper by means of an etching press. In time he perfected his technique, progressing from monotypes to which he added color after printing, to the last which are fully achieved in colors transferred from the plate to the paper by means of the press. These last monotypes, of which *Esterel Village* is one, comprise a group of landscapes made in 1890 and 1892 which stand apart from Degas' usual work in subject and in style. Said to have been done in recollection of the country Degas traveled through on a carriage trip to Burgundy and on train trips made in 1892, they are pure landscape, without human or animal life, which alone sets them apart from the main current of his work. They move closer to the abstract than any of his other works. During the years in which he made the late monotypes Degas was troubled with failing eyesight. This tragic development may in part account for Degas' radical change in subject, for the suppression of detail and the composition in masses of color which result in this luminous landscape, with its distant tower-accented hill and green fields glowing through the rosy atmosphere. L.S.R.

80 Mary Cassatt,
The Visitor,
soft ground etching
and aquatint

85 Honoré Daumier, *Sketches of Various Figures,* black chalk and gray ink wash

123 Karl Schmidt-Rottluff, *Self Portrait with Hat,* oil on canvas

117 Ernst Ludwig Kirchner, *Wrestlers in a Circus,* oil on canvas

OPPOSITE: Ernst Ludwig Kirchner (1880–1938) was the dominating figure of The Bridge (*Die Brücke*) movement founded in 1905 in Dresden. Along with the other original members of this group, Erich Heckel, Karl Schmidt-Rottluff, and Fritz Bleyl, Kirchner was a student of architecture. Inspired by the paintings of Vincent van Gogh and Edvard Munch as well as the graphic works of Rembrandt and Dürer, this group established the basis for modern German Expressionist art. At almost the same time as the Fauve artists in France the German artists began to work directly with broad areas of primary colors and violently distorted drawing. As the darker tones and ape-like figures in the background of *Wrestlers in a Circus* demonstrate, however, the Germans were less concerned with a decorative treatment of the canvas surface and more concerned with the expression of feelings and emotions about the world and especially society. This is one of the major canvases by Kirchner done in 1906, the year following the establishment of The Bridge movement. E.B.H.

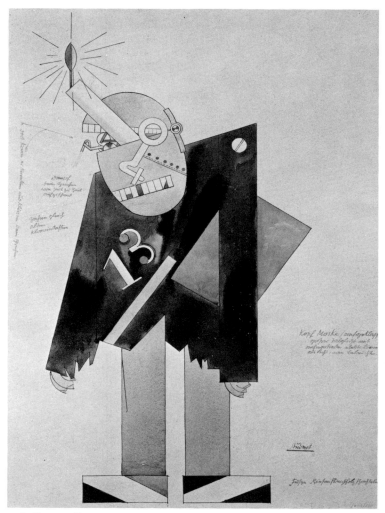

116 George Grosz,
Student (Study for Goll's "Methusalem"),
water color on paper

241

114 Sir Jacob Epstein, *The Weeping Woman*, bronze

93 Sir Jacob Epstein,
Sunita, conte crayon

113 Ernst Barlach,
Die Bettlerin,
terra cotta

120 Isamu Noguchi,
Woman with Child, white marble

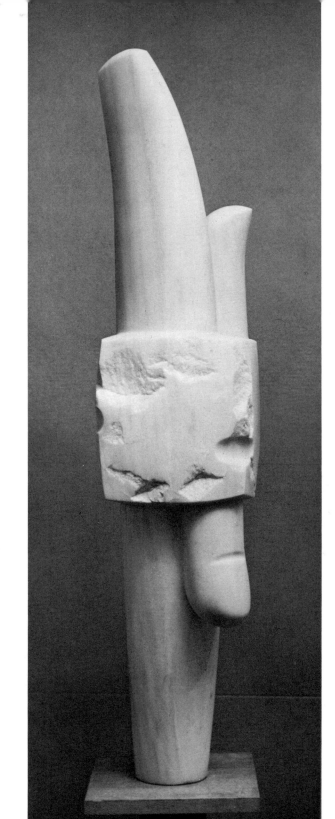

Isamu Noguchi was born in 1904 in Los
Angeles. His father was Japanese and his
mother American. He first studied sculpture with Gutzon Borglum and in 1927
and 1928 he was Brancusi's assistant in
Paris. During his stay in Europe he was influenced by Surrealism and especially by
Giacometti, Calder, and Miró. He has
also studied and worked in Japan, and his
sculpture is an exceptional blend of Eastern and Western elements. In 1958 he
executed *Woman with Child,* an abstract
marble sculpture with subtly curved and
polished vertical forms recalling the artist's
earlier association with Brancusi. Typical
of Noguchi, however, are the few unfinished, roughly textured areas contrasting
with the more highly finished surfaces. Noguchi is one of the very few contemporary
sculptors who still carves in marble; *Woman with Child* is one of his major works in
this medium. E.B.H.

119 Lucebert, *Nymphenfolies,*
oil on canvas

104 William Sommer,
The Lavender Horse,
pen and ink, water color

118 Richard Lindner,
Louis II, oil on canvas

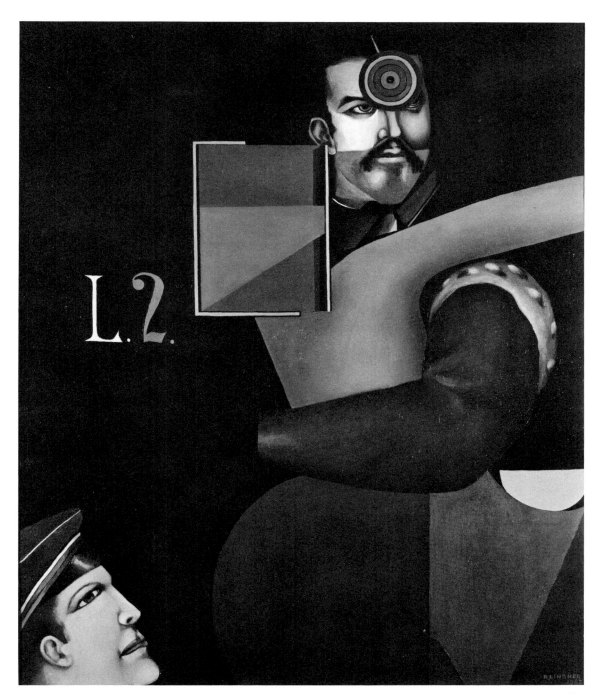

121 Irving Penn,
Colette, photograph

124 Adja Yunkers,
Untitled No. 2,
pastel on paper
mounted on board

115 Frank Gallo,
Male Image, epoxy rosin

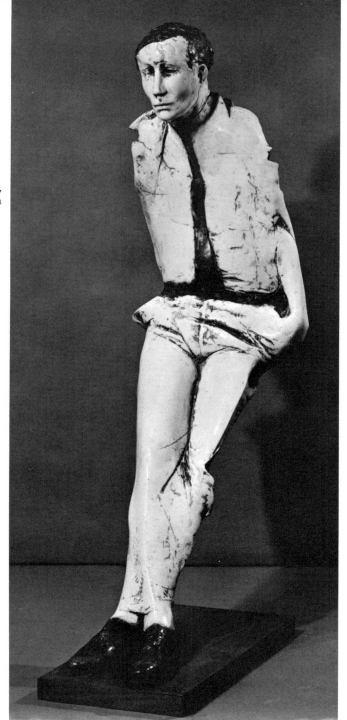

11 Charles Lakofsky,
Covered Jar,
porcelain

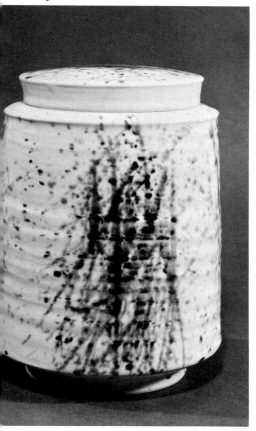

133 *Bodhisattva,* gray schist, India, Gandhara, 3rd century

OPPOSITE: This is the largest, most complete and striking early Indian metal image of the Buddha aside from the colossal Pala bronze in Birmingham. The use of inlays of silver in the eyes and of copper in the lips, the elegant proportions, the appearance of the base, and the composition of the brassy metal all point clearly to a Kashmiri origin. The extremely large size and high quality of the image, added to the still strong Gupta flavor of the head, body, and clinging drapery, place the figure at the high point of Kashmiri art, the reign of Lalitaditya, 700–ca.752, when Kashmir was a mighty empire extending from Tibet to the Indus and from Central Asia to the Deccan. The precise composition of the alloy is of considerable interest: copper 68.3%, zinc 20.2%, lead 11%, iron .25%, tin .10%. The very high and unusual percentage of lead is to be explained by the desire for a particularly fluid melt capable of easy pouring and accurate casting. This particular combination resulted in a lovely golden color with considerable apparent depth and softness. The fusion of this color with the physical representation and the flowing style produces a veritable epitome of the Buddha image—radiant, gracious, and compassionate. The special type of the image is particularly sacred—the Udayana Buddha, so named from the probably apocryphal but surely influential tale of the sandalwood statue magically made in the Buddha's lifetime for King Udayana of Kausambi. The image is somewhat worn from ritual touching mandatory in the adoring rite of worship. The slightly later incised inscription on the front of the base is in Western Tibetan script and attests to the importance and power of the image. A tentative reading is "Priest (Lha-Tsun) Nagaraja's private (or personal) image" (trans. Dr. P. Pal). It should be noted that Nagaraja is an Indian or Kashmiri name. S.E.L.

156 *Standing Buddha,*
brass, North India
or Kashmir,
early 8th century

140 *Devāta as Attendant Holding a Chauri,* red sandstone, India,
Kushan Period, Region of Mathura, 3rd century

132 Tao-chi (Shih-t'ao), Page from *Reminiscences of Ch'in-Huai River,*
eight-leaf album, ink and color on paper

254

OPPOSITE
142 *Gangā, Goddess of the Ganges,* stone,
India, Mathura, early 7th century

From Gupta times on, images of the two goddesses
personifying the sacred Ganges and Jumna rivers
were placed on either side of the entrances to temples
and shrines, notably in those Northern and Central
areas watered by the two rivers. Passing between the
two deities, the pilgrim was symbolically cleansed in
the holy waters personified by the two images. Since
the newly acquired sculpture shows the hip thrown
to the sinister side with the dexter hand hanging
freely, indicating a position on the dexter side of an
entrance, and since the feathery-tailed and lion-
clawed monster at the base represents a *makara* rather
than Jumna's tortoise, one can confidently identify
the figure as Gangā, the goddess of the Ganges. The
swelling and closely pressed breasts, full stomach, and
massive thighs, combined with the freely flowing,
feathery motifs of the *makara's* tail and such details
of jewelry as the pendant over the navel and the
girdle ornaments, indicate a date at the very beginning of the medieval period when Gupta motifs were
still in use. Sculptures of this period are exceedingly
rare outside of India, and this sensuous rendering of
womanly beauty is one of a very few sculptures which
give some idea of the style and quality of the best
works of a similar type at such famous sites as
Deogarh, Elephanta, Aurangabad, and Ellora. It
should be noted that the material is definitely the
mottled red and layered cream sandstone of the type
found in the quarries at Fatehpur Sikri and used in
the Mathura workshops. The sculptor has chosen a
block with a large outer layer of cream sandstone.
Thus the figure appears in this color, while the red
layers are hidden at the back of the high relief. s.e.l.

158 *Surya, the Sun God,*
brass, Kashmir, early 8th century

144 *A Guardian of Shiva,* stone, India, Hoysala Dynasty, Mysore, 13th century

145 *Head,* stone, India, Konarak, 13th century

139 *Dancing Tantric Figure,* stone stele, Nepal, 11th–12th century

134 *Bodhisattva Manjushri Jananasattva,* gilt bronze, Nepal, late 16th century

149 *Narrative Frieze: Life of a Hermit in Forest Retreat* (detail),
architrave from a Jain temple, wood with traces of color,
India, Gujarat, Jain, 16th–17th century

155 *Sita in the Garden of Lanka with Ravana and His Demons,*
The Siege of Lanka sequence from *The Ramayana,* gold and color on paper,
India, Rajputana, Punjab Hills, Guler, ca.1720

152 *Saint Seated in Yoga Posture,* ink and color on paper,
India, Punjab Hills, Basohli Style, ca.1700

147 *Krishna Stealing Milk,* strips of gold paper and color on paper,
India, Madura School, 18th century

146 *Krishna Destroying the Crane-Demon Bakāsura,*
strips of gold paper and color on paper,
India, Madura School, 18th century

137 *Comb Representing an Apsaras,*
ivory, Ceylon, 17th–18th century

264

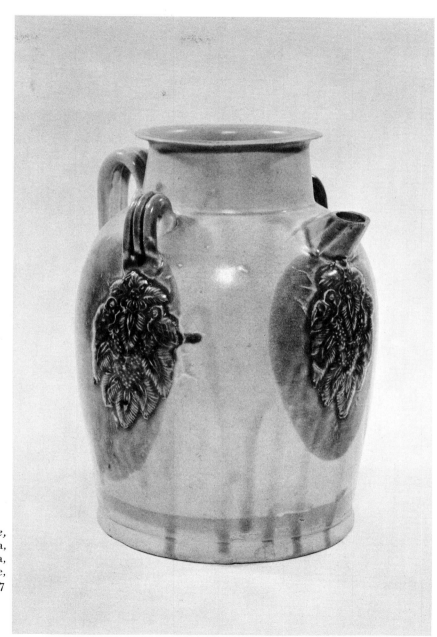

43 *Guardian Lion,*
white marble, China,
Sui or early T'ang Dynasty,
ca.600

141 *Ewer: T'ung-kuan ware,*
stoneware, China,
Wa-cha-p'ing, Ch'ang-sha,
Hu-nan Province,
early T'ang Dynasty, 618–907

51 *Potala Kuan-yin,*
wood (loquat),
China,
Five Dynasties Period,
10th century

148 *Lion: Yüeh ware,*
porcelain, China,
Northern Sung Dynasty,
960–1127

150 *Phoenix-headed Vase: Ch'ing-pai ware,*
porcelain, China, Northern Sung Dynasty, 960–1127

268

OPPOSITE: The present work is particularly rare in being a large hanging scroll of the twelfth century which combines the traditional Northern Sung monumental old tree subject with the more intimate Southern Sung academic bird and bush motif. The asymmetrical composition and the simplified profiles of the distant mountains are also progressive elements within the stylistic changes characteristic of the painting produced by the court painters in the new Southern Sung capital of Hangchou. The brushwork used in the cedar foliage and in the rocky cliff is highly individual and anticipates the handling of the famous thirteenth-century masters Ma Yüan and Hsia Kuei and of their lesser known but significant fourteenth-century follower, Wang Li. The painting has numerous seals, some of them now identified as those of the Prince of Chin (early Ming, ca.1400), Kêng Chaochung (a famous seventeenth-century collector) and Sung Lo (an equally famous and more discerning eighteenth-century connoisseur). On the nearest tree trunk there are an erased apocryphal signature and two seals which almost certainly read Wang Yüan, the most famous and sought-after fourteenth-century painter of birds, rock, and tree subjects, to whom was attributed almost any good anonymous painting in this category. The style, however, is obviously earlier. A second signature, still clearly visible, is on the dexter edge of the silk and reads Kao Tao. If this signature cannot command our complete confidence, it is singularly close to the mark, for Kao was a very obscure twelfth-century academician who was purportedly a specialist in finely rendered bird paintings and whose works are now totally unknown. Either the signature is good and this is indeed the first painting by Kao Tao to be revealed to us, or it is an added and canny attribution made by one of the previous owners of the scroll. The unusual eclectic character of the composition and the delicate brushwork of the details of birds and branches are characteristic of the early Southern Sung period as seen in such masters of the genre as Li Ti. One would search long and almost fruitlessly to find a comparable painting of this format, genre, and quality, even in the Palace Collections on Taiwan and the mainland. S.E.L.

131 Kao Tao (?),
*Birds in a Grove
in a Mountainous
Winter Landscape,*
ink and color on silk

270

153 *Shakyamuni*,
gilt bronze,
China,
Yüan Dynasty,
14th century

135 *Box with Cover,*
pierced porcelain,
five-color enamelled
ware, China,
Ming Dynasty,
Mark and Reign
of Wan Li, 1573–1619

154 *Shino ware Dish:
Nezumé* (mouse gray)
type, stoneware,
Japan,
Momoyama Period,
1573–1615

271

138 *Cosmetic Box,*
lacquer on wood, Japan,
Momoyama Period, 1596–1615

136 *Calligraphy by Koetsu Written over Designs by Sotatsu,* ink and gold,
silver on paper, Japan, early 17th century, Edo Period

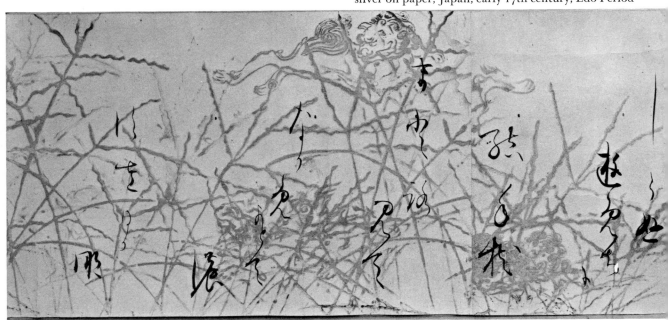

157 *Standing Figure of a Beauty: Kakiemon Type*, porcelain decorated in over-glaze colored enamels, Japan, Edo Period, late 17th century

159 *Teapot with Cover: Arita ware*, porcelain with colored enamel decoration, Japan, Edo Period, 1615–1868

274

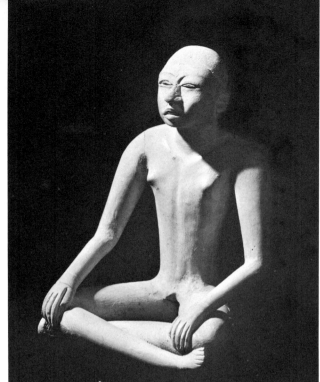

50 *Seated Figure,* terra cotta, Mexico, Northern Veracruz, Huastec, Panuco II

ILLUSTRATION WILLIAM M. HOLMES

49 *Seated Figure,* incised shell, Guatemala, Maya, 3rd–5th century

18 *Conch Shell,* earthenware, Western Mexico, Colima

275

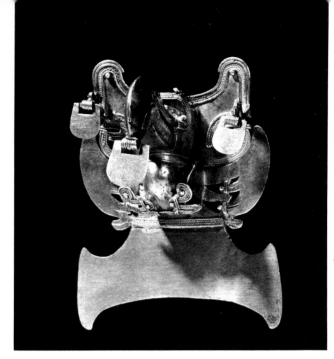

52 *Stylized Bird,* gold, Colombia,
Sinu, 13th century (?)

17 *Canoe Prow,* wood,
Southeast New Guinea,
Massim Area, Trobriand
Islands, 19th century

Catalogue

Objects are listed alphabetically by artist, if known, or by title. In listing the dimensions, height precedes width and depth.

EGYPTIAN AND CLASSICAL ART

1 Douris, Greek, Attic. *White-ground Lekythos.* Pottery, H. 12-3/4 inches, ca.500–490 B.C. Purchase, Leonard C. Hanna Jr. Bequest. 66.114

2 *Cameo of Zeus and Hera Seated Flanked by an Eros and Their Daughter Hebe.* Cameo shell, H. 3-1/4 inches. South Italy, 1st century B.C.
Collection: Dr. Philip Nelson, England.
Gift of Mr. and Mrs. J. J. Klejman. 66.131

3 *Cameo Representing Artemis.* Opaque glass, 1-1/2 x 1-5/8 inches. Italy, Roman, early 1st century A.D. (?).
Collection: Bronislaw Huberman, Poland.
Exhibited: Vienna, Kunsthistorisches Museum (extended loan).
Gift of Mr. and Mrs. J. J. Klejman. 65.465

4 *Figure of a Standing Lady.* Mainland (Peloponnesus) marble, H. 33-5/8 inches. Greece (from Alexandria?), ca.300 B.C. or later. John L. Severance Fund. 65.24

5 *Head of a Man.* Marble, H. 12-7/8 inches. Egypt, late 1st century B.C. to ca. A.D. 50.
Collection: Levi de Benzion, Paris.
Purchase from the J. H. Wade Fund. 66.20

6 *Octodrachnum.* Gold, Diam. 1-3/8 inches. Egypt. Dated K = year 10 reign of Ptolemaeus II or 261 B.C. The Norweb Collection. 65.552

DECORATIVE ARTS

7 Circle of Georg Raphael Donner, Austrian, 1692–1741. *House Altarpiece.* Gilded wood, 65 x 42-1/2 inches, ca.1740. Purchase, Leonard C. Hanna Jr. Bequest. 64.357

8 Modeled by Etienne-Maurice Falconet, French, Sèvres, 1716–1791. After a design by François Boucher, French, 1703–1770. *The Fête at the Château.* Porcelain, H. 8-1/4 inches, model executed 1766. The Norweb Collection 66.234

9 Giovanni Battista Foggini, Italian, Florence, 1652–1725. *David and Goliath.* Terra cotta, 16-1/4 x 18-3/4 x 12-3/8 inches, 1723. Gift of Harold T. Clark in Memory of Mrs. William B. Sanders. 66.126

10 Franz Ignaz Günther, German, Bavaria, 1725–1775. *Kneeling Angel.* Wood, H. 31-3/8 inches, ca.1760. John L. Severance Fund. 66.18

11 Charles L. Lakofsky, American, Cleveland, born 1922. *Covered Jar.* Porcelain, H. 7-3/4 inches, 1966. Wishing Well Fund. 66.221

12 Antonio Lopez (probably), Spanish, Leon. *Chalice.* Silver gilt, H. 11-11/16 inches. Dated 1732.
Collection: Monastery of Sobrado.
Andrew R. and Martha Holden Jennings Fund. 66.15

13 Joseph-Charles Marin, French, 1759–1834. *Bust of a Woman.* Terra cotta, H. 8 inches. Norman O. Stone and Ella A. Stone Memorial Fund. 66.16

14 Benjamin Pyne, English, 1684–1724. *Monteith.* Silver, Diam. 13-3/4 inches, H. 10-5/8 inches (with rim). Marked, dated 1715–16. Gift of Mr. and Mrs. Warren H. Corning. 65.467

15 Johann Andreas Thelot, German, Augsburg, 1654–1734. *Covered Cup.* Silver and gilt silver, H. 15-3/4 inches. Signed: J. A. Thelot f 1688. Purchase from the J. H. Wade Fund. 66.111

16 *Baptism of Christ.* Bronze, H. 24-3/4 inches. Italy, mid-17th century. Andrew R. and Martha Holden Jennings Fund. 65.471

17 *Canoe Prow.* Wood, 23-1/8 x 32-1/4 inches. Southeast New Guinea, Massim Area, Trobriand Islands, 19th century. Gift of Mr. and Mrs. J. J. Klejman. 66.130

18 *Conch Shell.* Earthenware, 5-3/8 x 8-3/4 x 10 inches. Western Mexico, Colima. Gift of J. H. Wade III. 66.127

19 *Cupid Carried by the Graces.* Porcelain, H. 10 inches. France, Sèvres, model executed 1768. After a design by François Boucher, French, 1703–1770. The Norweb Collection. 66.235

* * *

Faience. France. The Norweb Collection. 66.221–66.230:

20 *Bottle.* 2-3/16 x 5-3/4 x 7-7/8 inches. Marseilles, Fauchier Factory, ca.1745. 66.224

21 *Box in the Form of a Bunch of Asparagus.* 2-1/4 x 3-1/8 x 7 inches. Sceaux, ca.1765. 66.229

22 *Large Plate.* Diam. 17-3/8 inches. Nevers, ca.1700. 66.221

23 *Pair of Figures.* H. 11-1/8 and 11 inches. Strasbourg, 1745–1750. 66.225, 66.226

24 *Plate.* Diam. 9-7/8 inches. St. Omer, ca.1760–1770. 66.230

25 *Plate Decorated with Playing Cards.* Diam. 10-1/8 inches. Lille, ca.1750. 66.223

26 *Plate with Two Crayfish.* Diam. 8-3/4 inches. Strasbourg, 1750–1760. 66.227

27 *Round Box.* Faience with burled wood casing,

Diam. 4-11/16 inches, H. 2-3/16 inches. Moustiers, style of Orleys Factory, ca.1750. 66.222

28 *Tureen in the Form of a Turtle.* 6-7/8 x 8-5/8 x 12-1/2 inches. Strasbourg, 1750–1760. 66.228

* * *

29 *Incense Burner.* Terra cotta with traces of color, H. 41 inches. Mexico, Maya, Palenque Region, Classic, ca.A.D.500. Purchase from the J. H. Wade Fund. 65.248

30 *Intaglio.* Rock crystal with gilt-silver frame, 2 x 1-1/16 x 1/4 inches. Early Christian, 4th century. Inscribed: APITS EPS. Gift of Mr. and Mrs. J. J. Klejman. 65.464

31 *Kneeling Prophet.* Gilt bronze, H. 5-1/2 inches. Franco-Netherlands, ca. 1400.
Collection: Herbert Bier, London.
Purchase, Leonard C. Hanna Jr. Bequest. 64.360

* * *

Majolica. Italy:

32 *Albarello: Putto Riding a Wild Boar.* H. 8-7/8 inches. Siena (?), ca.1510.
Collection: Charles Damiron, Lyon.
Published: Charles Damiron, *Majoliques Italiennes,* n.d., No. 50, pl. XXIII.
Gift of the Twentieth Century Club. 65.553

33 *Plate: Horseman Riding a Unicorn.* Diam. 12-5/8 inches. Caffaggiolo, ca.1510.
Collection: Charles Damiron, Lyon.
Published: Charles Damiron, *Majoliques Italiennes* (n.d.), No. 75, pl. XXXIV.
Gift of Edgar A. Hahn. 66.129

34 *Plate with Lion.* Diam. 11-1/4 inches, H. 2-1/2 inches. Tuscany, second quarter 15th century.
Collection: Charles Damiron, Lyon.
Norman O. Stone and Ella A. Stone Memorial Fund. 66.19

35 *Plate with Profile Portrait of Young Man.* Sgraffito ware, Diam. 12-3/4 inches. Ca.1500.
Collection: Charles Damiron, Lyon.
Published: Charles Damiron, *Majoliques Italiennes* (n.d.), No. 45, pl. XXI.
Gift of Mr. and Mrs. Paul Damiron. 66.128

* * *

36 *Monogram of Christ (Chrismon).* Gold with garnets, 5-7/8 x 4-3/4 inches, Wt. 94 grams. Byzantium, Syria, 6th-7th century. Gift of Lillian M. Kern. 65.551

37 *Pot Pourri.* Porcelain, H. 6-3/8 inches. France, Vincennes, 1745–1750. The Norweb Collection. 66.233

* * *

Sculptures. Marble. East Mediterranean, late 3rd century. John L. Severance Fund. 65.237–65.247:

38 *Portrait Bust of a Woman.* 13-3/16 x 4 x 7-3/8 inches. 65.243

278

39 *Portrait Bust of a Woman.* 12-1/8 x 4-3/8 x 7-5/8 inches. 65.244

40 *Portrait Bust of a Woman.* 13-3/16 x 8 x 5 inches. 65.246

41 *The Good Shepherd.* 19-3/4 x 10-1/8 x 6-1/4 inches. 65.241

42 *Jonah Cast Up.* 16 x 8-1/2 x 14-13/16 inches. 65.238

43 *Jonah Swallowed by the Whale.* 20-5/16 x 6-1/8 x 10-5/16 inches. 65.237

44 *Jonah under the Gourd Vine.* 12-5/8 x 18-1/4 x 6-7/8 inches. 65.239

45 *Orant Figure (Jonah?).* 18-1/2 x 5-1/2 x 8-1/8 inches. 65.240

46 *Portrait Bust of a Man.* 13-1/8 x 8-1/4 x 5 inches. 65.242

47 *Portrait Bust of a Man.* 13-7/8 x 8-7/16 x 4-3/4 inches. 65.245

48 *Portrait Bust of a Man.* 13-5/16 x 8 x 4-3/8 inches. 65.247

* * *

49 *Seated Figure.* Incised shell, H. 6-1/2 inches. Guatemala, Maya, 3rd-5th century. The Norweb Collection. 65.550

50 *Seated Figure.* Terra cotta, H. 3-1/2 inches. Mexico, Northern Veracruz, Huastec, Panuco II, late 1st millenium B.C. James Albert and Mary Gardiner Ford Memorial Fund. 66.17

51 *Spoon.* Silver, silver gilt, and niello, L. 4-15/16 inches, Bowl 4-1/16 x 2-3/16 inches, Wt. 52.5 grams. Early Christian, 4th century. Inscribed: PAVLVS. John L. Severance Fund. 64.39

52 *Stylized Bird.* Gold, 2-1/2 x 3-1/8 inches. Colombia, Sinu, 13th century (?). In Memory of Mr. and Mrs. Henry Humphreys, Gift of their Daughter, Helen. 65.466

53 *Two Kneeling Carthusian Monks.* Marble, H. 10-1/8 and 9-1/2 inches. France, end of 14th century. *Collection:* Octave Homberg, Paris (?).
Exhibited: Baltimore, Walters Art Gallery, 1962: The International Style, no. 92 repr.
Published: Gaston Migeon, "Collection de M. Octave Homberg," *Les Arts,* III, No. 36 (December 1904), p. 36. Colin Eisler, "Le Gothique International," *Art de France,* IV (1964), p. 289, repr. John L. Severance Fund. 66.112, 66.113

PAINTINGS

54 Washington Allston, American, 1779–1843. *Portrait of Samuel Williams.* Oil on canvas, 56 x 44 inches, ca.1818.
Collections: Timothy Williams; Mrs. W. Pratt; Theodore Lyman, Brookline, Mass.; Mr. and Mrs. Lawrence A. Fleischman, Detroit.
Exhibited: Boston, Harding's Gallery, 1839. Boston, Museum of Fine Arts, 1881: Works of Art

Exhibited: Pt. 2, Paintings, Drawings, Engravings, and Decorative Art, cat. no. 203.
Published: Mabel Munson Swan, *The Atheneum Gallery 1827–1873* (Boston, 1940), p. 60, no. 62. E. P. Richardson, *Washington Allston* (Chicago, 1948), pp. 116, 117, 205, repr, pl. XLV. Mr. and Mrs. William H. Marlatt Fund. 65.474

55 Jean de Beaumetz, French, active 1361–died 1396. *The Calvary with a Carthusian Monk.* Oak Panel, 22-1/4 x 17-15/16 inches, ca.1390–1395.
Collections: La Chartreuse de Champmol, Dijon; Private collection in the vicinity of Dijon.
Exhibited: Musée de Dijon, Palais des Ducs de Bourgogne, 1960: La Chartreuse de Champmol, repr. pl. XX.
Published: Charles Sterling, "Oeuvres retrouvées de Jean de Beaumetz, Peintre de Philippe le Hardi," *Musées Royaux des Beaux-Arts Bulletin, Brussels,* IV (1955), 60-62, 68, 71, 72, 74, 78, 80, repr. p. 59. Millard Meiss and Colin Eisler, "A New French Primitive," *Burlington Magazine,* CII (1960), 234, 236. Michel Laclotte, "Peinture en Bourgogne au XVe Siècle," *Art de France,* No. 1 (1961), p. 289, n. 4. Albert Chatelet, *French Painting: from Fouquet to Poussin* (Geneva, 1963), p. 15. R. Guilly, *Kindlers Malerei Lexikon* (Zurich, 1964), Band (A-C), p. 257, repr. p. 256. William D. Wixom, "The Hours of Charles the Noble," CMA *Bulletin,* LII (March 1965) 83, n. 58. Purchase, Leonard C. Hanna Jr. Bequest. 64.454

56 Berlinghiero, Italian, Lucchese, active ca.1200–1240. *The Madonna and Child with Saints.* Triptych, poplar panels. Left shutter: *The Crucifixion of St. Andrew; St. Francis and St. Paul(?).* Right shutter: *The Last Judgment; SS. Stephen and Lawrence.* Exterior shutters: *Byzantine Cross.* Overall measurements of panels: 16-13/16 x 20-1/4 inches.
Collections: Theodore Bonjean, Paris; The Matthiesen Gallery, London; Adolphe Stoclet, Brussels; Mme. Michele Stoclet, Barcelona; (Sale, Sothéby, London, June 30, 1965, no. 21, repr.).
Published: Edward B. Garrison, Jr. "A Berlinghieresque Fresco in S. Stefano, Bologna," *Art Bulletin,* XXVIII (December 1946), 215 ff., repr. fig. 7. Garrison, "Post-War Discoveries—III: The Madonna 'Di Sotto Gli Organi,'" *Burlington Magazine,* LXXXIX (October 1947), 279. Garrison, *Italian Romanesque Panel Painting* (Florence, 1949), pp. 12, 112, no. 284. George Kaftal, *Iconography of the Saints in Tuscan Painting* (Florence, 1952), p. xxiii, n. 7, cols. 40, 613, 949. W. R. Valentiner, "A Madonna by Berlinghiero Berlinghieri," *North Carolina Museum of Art Bulletin,* I (Summer 1957), 3. Garrison, *Studies in the History of Medieval Italian Painting,* III (1957–1958) ("Addenda ad Indicem V" 1. A New Berlinghieresque Madonna), pp. 261-262, 264. James H. Stubblebine, *Guido da Siena* (Princeton, 1964), pp. 78, 88, repr. fig. 109.

Gift of The John Huntington Art and Polytechnic Trust. 66.237

57 Eugène Louis Boudin, French, 1825–1898. *Stormy Sky at Trouville.* Oil on canvas, 18-1/4 x 24 inches. Signed: L. Boudin Trouville.
Collection: Mr. and Mrs. Salmon P. Halle, Cleveland. Gift of Mrs. Abraham Strauss and S. Portland Halle II in Memory of Mr. and Mrs. Salmon P. Halle. 66.208

58 Robert Campin (The Master of Flémalle), Flemish, 1379–1444. *St. John the Baptist.* Oak panel, 6-13/16 x 4-13/16 inches.
Collections: Duc de Clermont-Tonnerre; Nettancourt-Vaubecourt Family (related to the former); Le Molt, Bourbonne-les-Bains; (Sale, Christie's, June 26, 1964, no. 44.).
Gift of The John Huntington Art and Polytechnic Trust. 66.238

59 Luca Giordano, Italian, Neapolitan, 1634–1705. *The Apparition of the Virgin to St. Francis of Assisi.* Oil on canvas, 94-1/2 x 77-1/4 inches, ca. 1681–1683.
Collections: Grand-Duke of Tuscany, Cosimo III; Private collection, Florence.
Published: Serie degli uomini i piu illustri nella pittura, scultura e architettura, con i loro elogi e ritratti (Florence, 1769–1775), Vol. XI, p. 208, n. 2.
Mr. and Mrs. William H. Marlatt Fund. 66.125

60 Giovanni di Paolo, Italian, Sienese, ca.1403–1482. *St. Catherine of Siena Invested with the Dominican Habit by SS. Dominic, Augustine, and Francis.* Panel, 11-3/8 x 9-1/16 inches, ca.1447–1449. *St. Catherine of Siena and the Beggar.* Panel, 11-5/16 x 11-3/8 inches, ca.1447–1449.
Collections: Johann Anton Ramboux (Sale, Cologne, May 23, 1867, Nos. 113 and 115); Adolphe Stoclet, Brussels; Mme. Michele Stoclet, Barcelona.
Published (selected bibliography): G. C. Carli, *Notizie de Belle Arti* (Ms. of about 1800–1810 in the Biblioteca Communale di Siena, c. vii–20), pp. 86 ff. J. A. Ramboux, *Katalog der Gemalde alter italienischer Meister (1221–1640) in der Sammlung des Conservator J. A. Ramboux* (Köln, 1862), nos. 113, 115. Bernhard Berenson, *Italian Pictures of the Renaissance* (Oxford, 1932), p. 245. John Pope-Hennessy, *Giovanni di Paolo* (London, 1937), pp. 130-135. Cesare Brandi, "Giovanni di Paolo—II," *Le Arti,* III, fasc. v (June-July 1941), 318 ff., pl. CXXI, fig. 29; pl. CXXII, fig. 31 (323, reconstruction). Margaretta Salinger, "A New Panel in Giovanni di Paolo's St. Catherine Series," *Bulletin of the Metropolitan Museum of Art,* N. S. 1 (Summer 1942), 26. Peleo Bacci, *Documenti i Commenti per la Storia dell'Arte,* (Florence, 1944), pp. 77-78. John Pope-Hennessy, "Giovanni di Paolo by Cesare Brandi: review," *Burlington Magazine,* LXXXIX (May 1947), 138-140. G. Kaftal, *St. Catherine in Tuscan Painting* (Ox-

ford, 1949), pp. 36-37, figs. VIII, XV. Gertrude Coor, "Quattrocento-Gemälde aus der Sammlung Ramboux," *Wallraf-Richartz-Jahrbuch*, XXI (1959), 82-85.
Gift of The John Huntington Art and Polytechnic Trust. 66.2, 66.3

61 Francisco José de Goya y Lucientes, Spanish, 1746–1828. *Portrait of the Infante Don Luis de Borbón*. Oil on canvas, 60-1/8 x 39-3/8 inches, 1783–1784.
Collections: Infante Don Luis Antonio Jaime de Borbón, Boadilla del Monte; Condes de Chinchon, Boadilla del Monte; Duque de Sueca, Conde de Chinchon; (Sale, February 7, 1914, Paris); Comte Mabou, Paris.
Exhibited: Paris, Musée Jacquemart-André, 1961–62: Francisco Goya y Lucientes, cat. no. 21, p. 30.
Published: Conde de la Viñaza, *Goya, Su Tiempo, Su Vida, Sus Obras* (Madrid, 1887), p. 228, no. 38. Paul Lafond, *Goya* (Paris, 1903), p. 120, no. 35. Valerian von Loga, *Francisco de Goya* (Berlin, 1903), pp. 43, 190, no. 144. Albert F. Calvert, *Goya* (London and New York, 1908), p. 128, no. 51. Hugh Stokes, *Francisco Goya* (New York, 1914), pp. 138, 328, no. 46. August L. Mayer, transl. Robert West, *Francisco de Goya* (London and Toronto, 1923), p. 148, no. 172. A. de Beruete y Moret, transl. Selwyn Brinton, *Goya as Portrait Painter* (London, Bombay, Sidney, 1922), p. 27. Antonina Vallentin, *Goya* (New York, 1949), p. 64. Xavière Desparmet Fitz-Gerald, *L'Oeuvre Peint de Goya* (Paris, 1928-1950), Vol. II, p. 32, no. 311.
Purchase, Leonard C. Hanna Jr. Bequest. 66.14

62 Jean Auguste Dominique Ingres, French, 1780–1867. *Antiochus and Stratonice*. Oil on canvas, 18-5/8 x 25 inches, ca.1834.
Collections: Mme. Ingres; Louis Bazille, Montpellier; Pierre Leenhardt; Alphonse Kann.
Published: Henri Delaborde, *Ingres, sa vie et ses travaux, sa doctrine, d'apres les notes manuscrites et les lettres du maître* (Paris, 1870), p. 220, no. 45. *Dictionnaire des Ventes d'Art* (Paris, 1911), p. 7, lot 6. Georges Wildenstein, *Ingres* (London, 1954), p. 210, no. 224, repr. fig. 181. Wolfgang Stechow, "Addenda to 'The Love of Antiochus with Faire Stratonica,'" *Bulletin du Musée National de Varsovie,* V (1964), 11. Mr. and Mrs. William H. Marlatt Fund. 66.13

63 Eastman Johnson, American, 1824–1906. *Portrait of Mr. Gineo Scott*. Oil on canvas, 40-1/4 x 50 inches. Signed and dated: E. J. Johnson 1859.
Collection: Family of Gineo Scott (until 1965).
Mr. and Mrs. William H. Marlatt Fund. 65.475

64 Bartolomé Esteban Murillo, Spanish, 1617-1682. *Laban Searching for His Stolen Household Gods in Rachel's Tent*. Oil on canvas, 95-1/2 x 142-1/2 inches, ca.1665–1670.
Collections: Marques de Villamanrique, Sevilla; Marques de Santiago, Santiago Palace, Madrid;

William Buchanan and W. G. Coesvelt, London (1809, acquired in Spain through William Buchanan's agent, G. Augustus Wallis); Marquis of Westminster, Grosvenor House, London; Hugh Richard Arthur Grosvenor, 2nd Duke of Westminster (the latter's grandson); (Sale: Christie, Manson and Woods, London, July 24, 1924, no. 21); Jacques de Canson, Paris; Carlos Guinle, Rio de Janeiro.
Published (selected bibliography): Antonio Palomino de Castro y Velasco, *El Museo Pictórico y Escala Optica* (1st ed.; Madrid, 1724), III, 424; (2nd ed.; Madrid, 1947), III, 1036. Richard Cumberland, *Anecdotes of Eminent Painters in Spain during the 16th and 17th Centuries* (London, 1787), II, 101-102, 124-125. J. Young, *A catalogue of the pictures at Grosvenor House* (London, 1820), p. 24, no. 69. William Buchanan, *Memoirs of Painting, with a Chronological History of the Importation of Pictures by the Great Masters into England since the French Revolution* (London, 1824), II, 221-222, 228-229, 233, 392. Charles B. Curtis, *Velazquez and Murillo* (London and New York, 1883), pp. 120-121, no. 10. W. Stirling Maxwell, *Annals of the Artists of Spain* (London, 1891), III, 1093–1094; IV, 1604. C. Justi, *Murillo* (2nd ed.; Leipzig, 1904), p. 14. Albert F. Calvert, *Murillo* (London and New York, 1907), pp. 155-156. August L. Mayer, *Murillo* (Klassiker der Kunst) (Stuttgart and Berlin, 1913), p. XIX, repr. p. 107. August L. Mayer, "Murillo," *Thieme-Becker, Allgemeines Lexikon der bildenden Kunstler* (Leipzig, 1931), XXV, 286. L. Réau, *Iconographie de l'art chrétien* (Paris, 1956), II, 150. J. A. Gaya Nuño, *La Pintura Española fuera de España* (Madrid, 1958), p. 250, no. 1945. G. Kubler and M. Soria, *Art and Architecture in Spain and Portugal* (Baltimore, 1959), p. 277.
Gift of the John Huntington Art and Polytechnic Trust. 65.469

65 Jusepe de Ribera, Spanish, 1591–1652. *The Death of Adonis*. Oil on canvas, 73 x 94 inches, ca.1635–1639.
Collections: Mr. Bartolomi, Château de Versoi, near Geneva; La Comtesse de Rougé (the former's granddaughter); (Sale: Christie's, April 1, 1960, no. 101, repr. pl. LIII).
Mr. and Mrs. William H. Marlatt Fund. 65.19

66 Gabriel de Saint-Aubin, French, 1724–1780. *Laban Cherchant ses Dieux*. Oil on canvas, 17-15/16 x 21-5/8 inches, ca.1753.
Reference: E. Dacier, "Une peinture retrouvée de Gabriel de Saint-Aubin, Laban cherchant ses Dieux," *Gazette des Beaux-Arts*, 6. per., XIV (1935), 42 ff. (without knowledge of the Cleveland sketch).
Gift of Ruth and Sherman E. Lee in Memory of Their Parents, George B. Ward, Emery and Adelia Lee. 65.548

67 Adriaen van de Velde, Dutch, 1636–1672. *Land-scape with Sleeping Shepherdess.* Oil on wood, 18-15/16 x 10-13/16 inches. Signed and dated: A. v. Velde 1663.
Collection: Arthur C. Tate.
Mr. and Mrs. William H. Marlatt Fund. 66.12

PRINTS AND DRAWINGS

68 Kenneth Armitage, English, born 1916. *Study for Sculpture.* Brush and black ink, 15-1/8 x 20-1/8 inches. Signed and dated: KA '53. Gift of Mr. and Mrs. George M. Reid. 65.457

69 Hans Baldung (called Grien), German, 1484/85–1545. *Adam and Eve.* Woodcut, 10-1/16 x 3-13/16 inches, Hollstein II.75.2, only state. Dated: 1519. Dudley P. Allen Fund. 66.6

70 Hans Baldung (called Grien). *The Bewitched Groom.* Woodcut, 13-3/8 x 7-7/8 inches, 1544, Hollstein II.139.237, state I/II.
Collections: Dr. Julius Hofmann, Carlsbad and Vienna; E. A. Seasongood, New York.
Exhibited: The Minneapolis Institute of Arts, 1956: Prints 1400–1800 (also Cleveland and Chicago). The Baltimore Museum of Art, 1966: Italian and Northern Renaissance Prints.
Mr. and Mrs. Charles G. Prasse Collection, Fiftieth Anniversary Gift. 66.172

71 Leonard Baskin, American, born 1922. *Adolf Menzel.* Etching, 17-13/16 x 15-1/8 inches. Signed: Baskin. Anonymous Gift. 66.155

72 Leonard Baskin. *Marigolds.* Etching and aquatint printed in black and green, 17-3/4 x 14-5/8 inches. Signed: Baskin. Gift of Park Synagogue Festival Committee. 66.170

73 Nicolas Beatrizet, French, active in Rome 1540–1565. *La Chute de Phaéton.* Engraving, 16-1/2 x 11-7/16 inches, Robert-Dumesnil IX.151.31, state I/II.
Collection: Albert Maroni, Paris.
Gift of Mr. and Mrs. Richard H. Zinser. 65.458

74 Domenico Beccafumi, Italian, 1486–1551. Page from a Sketch Book: *The Head of a Woman* (recto), *A Kitchen Maid* (verso). Black chalk, 8-1/2 x 5-3/4 inches, before 1512.
Collections: George Hibbert, London; Coghlan Briscoe, London; Dr. W. M. Crofton.
Exhibited: London, Thos. Agnew & Sons, Ltd., 1965: Domenico Beccafumi . . . Drawings from a Sketchbook.
Published: R. de Liphart Rathshoff, "Un Libro di Schizzi di Domenico Beccafumi," *Rivista d'Arte*, XVII (1935), 41-43, 59, figs. 3, 17. L. E. Holden Fund. 66.120

75 Max Beckmann, German, 1884–1950. *Woman with Candle.* Woodcut, 11-13/16 x 5-13/16 inches, 1920, Glaser 149, state II/II. Gift of Henry H. Hawley. 66.160

76 Hieronymus Bosch, Flemish, ca.1450–1516. *Two Blind Men (The Blind Leading the Blind).* Engraving, 8-7/8 x 10-3/16 inches, Hollstein III.138.21, state I/V. (Engraved by Pieter van der Heyden.) Delia E. Holden Fund. 66.11

77 Charles E. Burchfield, American, born 1893. *The Sunflower Arch.* Indelible pencil and crayons, 19-7/8 x 13-7/8 inches. Signed with monogram. Dated: 1917.
Exhibited: The Cleveland Museum of Art, 1953: The Drawings of Charles E. Burchfield. Whitney Museum of American Art, 1956: Charles Burchfield.
Mr. and Mrs. Charles G. Prasse Collection. 65.461

78 Charles E. Burchfield. *Deserted House.* Brush and India ink, water color and crayons, 13-3/4 x 19-3/8 inches. Signed with monogram. Dated: 1923.
Exhibited: The Cleveland Museum of Art, 1953: The Drawings of Charles E. Burchfield. Whitney Museum of American Art, 1956: Charles Burchfield.
Mr. and Mrs. Charles G. Prasse Collection. 65.462

79 Luca Cambiaso, Italian, 1527–1585. *Apollo Flaying Marsyas.* Pen and brown ink and ink wash, 12-1/8 x 8-1/2 inches.
Collection: Mrs. M. M. Wells, Sheffield.
The Norweb Collection, Fiftieth Anniversary Gift. 66.169

80 Mary Cassatt, American, 1845–1926. *The Visitor.* Soft ground etching and aquatint, 15-3/4 x 12-1/8 inches, ca.1881, Breeskin 34, between state II and III/V.
Collection: Edgar Degas, Paris.
Gift of Fifty Members of The Print Club of Cleveland on the Occasion of the Fiftieth Anniversary. 66.176

81 Frans Crabbe, Flemish, ca.1480–1553. *Adoration of the Shepherds.* Engraving, 9-5/8 x 6-15/16 inches, ca.1522–25, Hollstein V.68.6.
Collection: Lord Northwick.
Purchase from the J. H. Wade Fund. 66.121

82 Nathaniel Currier, American, 1813–1888. *American Farm Scenes, No. 4 (Winter).* Lithograph colored by hand, 16-11/16 x 23-7/8 inches (border line), 1853, Peters 2309. In Memory of Harold T. Clark, Gift of Mrs. Harold T. Clark. 65.525

83 Honoré Daumier, French, 1808–1879. *L'Histoire ancienne: l'abandon d'Ariane.* Lithograph, 9-1/2 x 8 inches, 1842, Delteil 948, state III/IV. Mr. and Mrs. Charles G. Prasse Collection. 65.543

84 Honoré Daumier. *L'Histoire ancienne: les écuries d'Augias.* Lithograph, 9-13/16 x 8-3/16 inches, 1842, Delteil 950, state III/III. Mr. and Mrs. Charles G. Prasse Collection. 65.544

85 Honoré Daumier. *Sketches of Various Figures.* Black chalk and gray ink wash (verso: pen and ink, black chalk, ink and water-color wash), 2-5/8 x 11-13/16 inches.

Collections: Richard S. Davis, Minneapolis; E. Powis Jones, New York.
Fiftieth Anniversary Gift of Mr. and Mrs. Eugene Victor Thaw. 66.179

86 Edgar Degas, French, 1834–1917. *Esterel Village.* Monotype, 11-13/16 x 16-3/4 inches, ca.1890–1892.
Collections: Maurice De Gas; Maurice Exsteens; Private collection, Switzerland.
Exhibited: New York, E. V. Thaw & Co., 1964: 9 Monotypes by Degas.
Fiftieth Anniversary Gift of The Print Club of Cleveland. 66.177

87 Nikolaus Manuel Deutsch I, Swiss, ca.1484–1530. *The Fifth Foolish Virgin.* Woodcut, 7-1/4 x 4-3/16 inches, Hollstein VI.193.10. Dated: 1518. Cornelia Blakemore Warner Fund. 66.8

88 Lambert Doomer, Dutch, 1622/23–1700. *View of Orleans on the Loire.* Pen and brown ink, brown and gray washes, 9-3/8 x 16-3/16 inches. Inscribed (on back): De Stad Orlejens aan de rivier de Loore.
Collections: J. Tonneman, Amsterdam; Wacker van Zon; H. E. ten Cate, Oldenzaal, Netherlands.
Exhibited: Amsterdam, Rijksmuseum, 1936: Oude Kunst.
Published: D. Hannema, *Catalogue of the H. E. ten Cate Collection* (Rotterdam, 1955) no.199, pl.107. H. M. van den Berg, "Willem Schellinks en Lambert Doomer in Frankrijk," *Oudheidkundig Jaarboek*, XI (1942), p.29, no.70, repr. pl.28. Delia E. Holden Fund. 66.4

89 Albrecht Dürer, German, 1471–1528. *The Arm of Eve.* Brush and brown ink heightened with white on blue Venetian paper, 13-3/16 x 10-1/2 inches. Signed with monogram. Dated: 1507.
Collections: Joseph Grünling, Vienna; A. Ritter von Franck, Vienna and Graz; Amsler & Ruthardt, Berlin; Albertina, Vienna; Archduke Friedrich of Austria, Vienna.
Published: Joseph Heller, *Das Leben und die Werke Albrecht Dürers* (Leipzig, 1831), p.125, no.24. Friedrich Lippmann, *Zeichnungen von Albrecht Dürer*, II (Berlin, 1888), p.19, no.164, repr. in facsimile. Eduard Flechsig, *Albrecht Dürer*, II (Berlin, 1931), p.570, no. 519. Friedrich Winkler, *Die Zeichnungen Albrecht Dürers*, II (Berlin, 1937), p.113, no.434, repr. Hans Tietze and Erika Tietze-Conrat, *Kritisches Verzeichnis der Werke Albrecht Dürers*, II, part 1 (Basel, 1937), p.38, no.348, repr. p.190. Erwin Panofsky, *Albrecht Dürer*, II (Princeton, 1948), p.20, no. 1208.
Accessions Reserve Fund. 65.470

90 Albrecht Dürer. *The Holy Family with Two Musician Angels.* Woodcut, 8-7/16 x 8-3/8 inches, Meder 216, proof a/d. Dated: 1511.
Collection: J. H. Bender, Kansas City, Missouri.
Gift of William Ellery Greene for the Lucy S. Greene Collection. 65.538

91 Albrecht Dürer. *St. Jerome in Penitence.* Engraving, 12-5/8 x 8-13/16 inches, ca.1497, Dodgson 11.
Collection: Prince of Liechtenstein.
Mr. and Mrs. Charles G. Prasse Collection, Fiftieth Anniversary Gift. 66.175

92 Anthony van Dyck, Flemish, 1599–1641. *The Lamentation.* Black chalk, brush and ink, heightened with white, on gray paper, 16-13/16 x 18-5/8 inches.
Collection: Johannes Noll.
Mr. and Mrs. Charles G. Prasse Collection, Fiftieth Anniversary Gift. 66.174

93 Sir Jacob Epstein, English (born in U.S.A.), 1880–1959. *Sunita.* Conte crayon, 17-7/16 x 21-7/8 inches, 1928. Signed: Epstein. Gift of The Louis D. Beaumont Foundation. 66.152

94 Sir Jacob Epstein. *Sunita.* Pencil and water color, 17-1/4 x 22-1/2 inches, ca.1932–33. Signed: Epstein. Gift of The Louis D. Beaumont Foundation. 66.151

95 Jean Baptiste Isabey. French, 1767–1855. *Voyage en Italie en 1822.* Bound album of 30 lithographs, 14-1/8 x 9-3/4 inches (page), 1833, Basily-Callimaki 243-273, published state. Gift of Harold T. Clark in Memory of Mrs. William B. Sanders. 66.218

96 Master H L, German, active 1510–ca.1533. *Angels Carrying the Emblems of the Passion.* Engraving, 5-1/4 x 3-3/4 inches, Lossnitzer (Leinberger) 7, state II/II. Dated: 1533.
Collection: Albertina, Vienna.
Dudley P. Allen Fund. 66.5

97 Samuel Palmer, English, 1805–1881. *The Vine.* Etching with pencil corrections, 11-3/4 x 8-3/4 inches (page), ca.1852, Griggs & Alexander 5, state III/IV. Signed, and inscribed with the artist's penciled notes.
Collections: A. H. Palmer; J. H. Bender, Kansas City, Missouri.
Exhibited: London, Victoria and Albert Museum, 1926: Drawings, Etchings and Woodcuts by Samuel Palmer and other Disciples of William Blake.
Mr. and Mrs. Lewis B. Williams Collection, Presented in Honor of Henry Sayles Francis, Curator of Prints. 66.185

98 Samuel Palmer. *The Morning of Life.* Etching and drypoint, 5-3/8 x 8-3/16 inches (etched design), begun 1860–61, Griggs & Alexander 10, between state II and III/VI. Signed: Samuel Palmer.
Collection: J. H. Bender, Kansas City, Missouri.
Mr. and Mrs. Lewis B. Williams Collection, Presented in Honor of Henry Sayles Francis, Curator or Prints. 66.194

99 Samuel Palmer. *The Lonely Tower.* Etching, 6-1/2 x 9-1/8 inches (etched design), 1879, Griggs & Alexander 12, state I/VI.
Collections: A. H. Palmer; J. H. Bender, Kansas City, Missouri.

Exhibited: London, Victoria and Albert, 1926: Drawings, Etchings and Woodcuts by Samuel Palmer and other Disciples of William Blake. Mr. and Mrs. Lewis B. Williams Collection, Presented in Honor of Henry Sayles Francis, Curator of Prints. 66.199

100 Samuel Palmer. *The Cypress Grove.* Etching, 3-15/16 x 5-15/16 inches, 1876, Griggs & Alexander 15, state I/IV.
Collection: J. H. Bender, Kansas City, Missouri.
Mr. and Mrs. Lewis B. Williams Collection, Presented in Honor of Henry Sayles Francis, Curator of Prints. 66.204

101 Prince Rupert von der Pfalz, German, 1619–1682. *Standard Bearer.* Mezzotint, 11-3/16 x 7-15/16 inches (paper), Russell II.487.5, state I/III. Dated: 1658.
Collections: Pierre Mariette, Paris (1667); Lloyd-Baker.
Dudley P. Allen Fund. 66.10

102 Gabriel de Saint-Aubin, French, 1724–1780. *Fête in a Park with Costumed Dancers.* Ink, ink and water-color washes, over pencil indications, 7-13/16 x 12-5/16 inches, ca.1760–65.
Collection: John S. Thacher.
Exhibited: Pittsburgh, Carnegie Institute, 1951: French Painting 1100–1900.
Purchase from the J. H. Wade Fund. 66.124

* * *

William Sommer, American, 1867–1949. Six drawings. Gift of Dr. and Mrs. Theodor W. Braasch:

103 *Apples.* Pen and ink, 4 x 5-15/16 inches. 65.516

104 *The Lavender Horse.* Pen and ink, water color, 15-15/16 x 12-7/16 inches. 65.522

105 *Mrs. Sommer's Goat.* Pen and ink, 4-5/16 x 7 inches, ca.1938. 65.518

106 *Sketch for Geneva Post Office Mural.* Pen and ink, water color and gouache, squared, 9-1/4 x 19-9/16 inches, 1938. Signed: Wm Sommer. 65.521

107 *Two Apples.* Pencil, 7-3/4 x 9-15/16 inches. Signed: Wm Sommer. 65.520

108 *The Valley Farm.* Pencil, pen and ink, water color, 12-9/16 x 7-7/16 inches. Signed: Wm Sommer. 65.524

* * *

109 Philipp Uffenbach, German, 1566–1636. *The Resurrection.* Etching, 9-13/16 x 8-3/16 inches, Andresen IV.2.2, state I/II. Dated: 1588. Dudley P. Allen Fund. 66.122

110 Adriaen van de Velde, Dutch, 1636–1672. *Seated Peasant Woman.* Red chalk, 7-3/16 x 9-3/16 inches.
Collection: Léon Suzor, Paris.
Exhibited: Paris, Musée Carnavalet, 1950: Chefs-d'oeuvre des collections parisiennes.
John L. Severance Fund. 66.239

111 Esaias van de Velde, Dutch, ca.1590–1630. *Hilly Landscape with House beside a Stream.* Black chalk with tan and gray washes, 7-11/16 x 11-1/2 inches. Signed and dated: E. V. Velde 1627.
Collections: August Grahl, Dresden; Staedelsches Kunstinstitut Frankfurt; H. E. ten Cate, Oldenzaal, Netherlands.
Published: D. Hannema, *Catalogue of the H. E. ten Cate Collection* (Rotterdam, 1955), no. 298.
Dudley P. Allen Fund. 66.7

112 Enea Vico, Italian, 1523–1567. *Ewer Ornamented with Dolphins.* Engraving, 9-9/16 x 7-3/16 inches, Bartsch XV.352.432. Dated: 1543. Gift of Leona E. Prasse in Memory of Mrs. Ralph M. Coe. 66.173

CONTEMPORARY ART

113 Ernst Barlach, German, 1870–1938. *Die Bettlerin.* Terra cotta, 11-1/2 x 12-3/4 x 8-1/2 inches. Gift of William Mathewson Milliken in Memory of Mr. and Mrs. Ralph M. Coe. 66.142

114 Sir Jacob Epstein, English (born in U.S.A.), 1880–1959. *The Weeping Woman.* Bronze (second cast of edition of six), 23-1/4 x 16-1/2 x 19 inches, 1922.
Exhibited: Leicester Galleries, 1924: At the City of Leicester Art Galleries.
Published: Robert Black, *The Art of Jacob Epstein* (Cleveland: World, 1942), pp. 62, 234, pl. 15. Stanley Casson, *Some Modern Sculptors* (London: Oxford University Press, 1928), p. 114. Roger Fry, *Transformations* (London: William Chase & Sons, 1926), p. 138. Jacob Epstein, *Let There Be Sculpture* (New York: G. P. Putnam's Sons, 1940), p. 364. Jacob Epstein, as told to Arnold L. Haskell, *The Sculptor Speaks* (New York: Doubleday, Doran & Co., 1932), p. 187.
Gift from the Louis Dudley Beaumont Foundation. 66.140

115 Frank Gallo, American, born 1933. *Male Image.* Epoxy rosin (number one in an edition of five), 63 x 20 x 31 inches, base: 2 x 4 x 31 inches, 1965. Contemporary Collection. 66.1

116 George Grosz, American (born in Germany), 1893–1959. *Student* (Study for Goll's "Methusalem"). Water color on paper, 20-1/2 x 14-1/2 inches, 1922. Contemporary Collection. 66.50

117 Ernst Ludwig Kirchner, German, 1880–1938. *Wrestlers in a Circus.* Oil on canvas, 31-3/4 x 37 inches, 1906.
Published: Will Grohmann, *Das Werk Ernst Ludwig Kirchner* (Munich: Kurt Wolff Verlag, 1926), repr. no. 63. Bernard Myers, *Kirchner* (New York: Fine Arts Associates, 1957), cat. no. 4.
Contemporary Collection and Bequest of William R.Valentiner. 66.49

118 Richard Lindner, American, born (in Germany) 1901. *Louis II.* Oil on canvas, 50 x 40 inches, 1962.
Collection: Arne H. Ekstrom, New York.

Exhibited: The Cleveland Museum of Art, 1966: Fifty Years of Modern Art.
Published: Edward B. Henning, *Fifty Years of Modern Art* (The Cleveland Museum of Art, 1966), p. 150.
Contemporary Collection. 65.450

119 Lucebert, Dutch, born 1924. *Nymphenfolies.* Oil on canvas, 27-3/4 x 35-5/8 inches, 1960. Gift of Mrs. Gordon D. Meals. 66.139

120 Isamu Noguchi, American, born 1904. *Woman with Child.* White marble, H. 44 inches, base: H. 37-1/2 inches, 1958.
Exhibited: The Cleveland Museum of Art, 1966: Fifty Years of Modern Art.
Published: Edward B. Henning, *Fifty Years of Modern Art* (The Cleveland Museum of Art, 1966), p. 135.
Contemporary Collection. 66.48

121 Irving Penn, American, born 1917. *Colette.* Photograph, black and white, 22 x 21-7/8 inches, 1951.
Exhibited: New York, World's Fair, 1965: Photography in the Fine Arts.
Gift of the artist. 66.141

122 Hugo Robus, American, 1885–1964. *Woman Combing Her Hair.* Bronze (fourth casting), 15-3/4 x 18-1/2 x 14 inches. Gift of Hugo Robus, Jr., in Memory of his Father, Hugo Robus. 66.51

123 Karl Schmidt-Rottluff, German, born 1884. *Self Portrait with Hat.* Oil on canvas, 28-7/8 x 25-5/8 inches, 1919
Collection: William R. Valentiner, Raleigh.
Bequest of William R. Valentiner. 65.440

124 Adja Yunkers, American, born 1900. *Untitled No. 2.* Pastel on paper mounted on board, 46-1/2 x 68-1/2 inches, 1961.
Contemporary Collection. 66.138

NEAR EASTERN ART

125 *Beaker.* Gold, repoussé and engraved, H. 5-1/2 inches. Northwestern Iran (said to have been found at Marlik), ca.1000 B.C.
Exhibited: Paris, Petit Palais, 1961–62: Sept mille ans d'art en Iran.
Published: Sept mille ans d'art en Iran (exh. cat.; Paris: Petit Palais, 1961), pl. VII.
Purchase from the J. H. Wade Fund. 65.26

126 *Ewer.* Gold, H. 4-3/4 inches. Iran, Buyid Period. Inscribed with the name Samsam al-Dawla [985–998].
Published: Gaston Wiet, *Soieries Persanes* (Cairo, 1948), p. 91, pl. xx. Ernst Kühnel, "Die Kunst Persiens unter den Buyiden," *Zeitschrift der Deutschen Morgenländischen Gesellschaft,* CVI, 1 (N.S. XXXI) (Wiesbaden, 1956), pp. 78-92, pl. II, 6.
Purchase from the J. H. Wade Fund. 66.22

127 *Ewer.* Silver, H. 14 inches. Iran, Sasanian Period,

probably 5th-6th century A.D. Purchase from the J. H. Wade Fund. 66.21

128 *Finial in Form of an Ibex Protome.* Cast bronze, H. 8-3/4 inches. Iran, Luristan, late 7th century B.C.
Published: D.G. Shepherd, "A Bronze Sculpture from Iran," CMA *Bulletin* (December 1961), p. 258, fig. 7.
Gift of the Junior Council of The Cleveland Museum of Art. 65.554

129 *Rhyton: The Angel Dravspa.* Silver, repoussé and engraved, partially gilded, H. 7-1/2 inches. Iran (?), Sasanian Period, 4th–5th century. Purchase, Leonard C. Hanna Jr. Bequest. 64.96

130 *Textile Fragment.* Silk, 25 x 18-3/4 inches. Iran, Buyid Period, 10th–11th century.
Published: Gaston Wiet, *Soieries Persanes* (Cairo, 1948), p. 72-78, pl. xv.
Purchase from the J. H. Wade Fund. 66.23

ORIENTAL ART

131 Kao Tao (?), Chinese, Sung Dynasty, 12th century. *Birds in a Grove in a Mountainous Winter Landscape.* Ink and color on silk, 68-7/8 x 35-1/2 inches. John L. Severance Fund. 66.115

132 Tao-chi (Shih-t'ao), Chinese, before 1645—after 1704, Ch'ing Dynasty. *Reminiscences of Ch'in-Huai River.* 8-leaf album, ink and color on paper, 10-1/16 x 7-15/16 inches.
Published: Victoria Contag, *Die Beiden Steine* (Braunschweig: Verlagsanstalt Hermann Klemm, 1950), pls. 5-8.
John L. Severance Fund. 66.31

133 *Bodhisattva.* Gray schist, H. 52-1/8 inches. India, Gandhara, 3rd century A.D. Purchase from the J. H. Wade Fund. 65.476

134 *Bodhisattva Manjushri Jananasattva.* Gilt bronze, H. 30-3/4 inches. Nepal, late 16th century. Purchase, Leonard C. Hanna Jr. Bequest. 64.370

135 *Box with Cover.* Pierced porcelain, five-color enamelled ware, 7-3/16 x 9-15/16 inches. China, Ming Dynasty, Mark and Reign of Wan Li, 1573–1619.
Published: Sekai toji zenshu (Catalogue of World's Ceramics), vol. XI (Tokyo 1955), pl. 117.
John L. Severance Fund. 66.117,a

136 *Calligraphy by Koetsu Written over Designs by Sotatsu.* Ink and gold, silver on paper, 9-1/8 x 136-1/2 inches. Japan, early 17th century, Edo Period. John L. Severance Fund. 66.118

137 *Comb Representing an Apsaras.* Ivory, 4-1/8 x 3-5/8 inches. Ceylon, 17th–18th century. Gift of Robert Rousset. 66.148

138 *Cosmetic Box.* Lacquer on wood, 10-1/2 x 13-1/8 inches. Japan, Momoyama Period, 1596–1615. Andrew R. and Martha Holden Jennings Fund. 66.25

139 *Dancing Tantric Figure.* Stone stele, H. 3-3/4 inches. Nepal, 11th–12th century. Gift of Claude de Marteau. 66.144

140 *Devāta as Attendant Holding a Chauri.* Red sandstone, H. 22 inches. India, Kushan Period, Region of Mathura, 3rd century. Andrew R. and Martha Holden Jennings Fund. 65.472

141 *Ewer: T'ung-kuan ware.* Stoneware, H. 8-7/8 inches. China, Wa-cha-p'ing, Ch'ang-sha, Hu-nan Province, early T'ang Dynasty, 618–907. Gift of N. V. Hammer. 66.145

142 *Gangā, Goddess of the Ganges.* Stone, H. 42-1/2 inches. India, Mathura, early 7th century. John L. Severance Fund. 66.119

143 *Guardian Lion.* White marble, H. 31 inches. China, Sui or early T'ang Dynasty, ca. A.D. 600. Purchase from the J. H. Wade Fund. 65.473

144 *A Guardian of Shiva.* Stone, H. 44-5/8 inches. India, Hoysala Dynasty, Mysore, 13th century. John L. Severance Fund. 64.369

145 *Head.* Stone, H. 4-3/16 inches. India, Konarak, 13th century. Gift of Robert Rousset. 66.147

146 *Krishna Destroying the Crane-Demon Bakāsura.* Strips of gold paper and color on paper, 10-7/8 x 7-11/16 inches. India, Madura School, 18th century. John L. Severance Fund. 66.29

147 *Krishna Stealing Milk.* Strips of gold paper and color on paper, 10-7/8 x 7-5/8 inches. India, Madura School, 18th century. John L. Severance Fund. 66.28

148 *Lion: Yüeh ware.* Porcelain, H. 7-1/8 inches. China, Northern Sung Dynasty, 960–1127. Fanny Tewksbury King Collection, by exchange 66.26

149 *Narrative Frieze: Life of a Hermit in Forest Retreat, Architrave from a Jain Temple.* Wood, with traces of color, 8 x 100-1/2 inches. India, Gujarat, Jain, 16th–17th century. Gift of George P. Bickford. 65.555

150 *Phoenix-headed Vase: Ch'ing-pai ware.* Porcelain, H. 15-3/8 inches. China, Northern Sung Dynasty, 960–1127. Mr. and Mrs. Severance A. Millikin Collection. 65.468

151 *Potala Kuan-yin.* Wood (loquat), H. 5-15/16 inches. China, Five Dynasties Period, 10th century. Gift of Mrs. A. Dean Perry. 65.556

152 *Saint Seated in Yoga Posture.* Ink and color on paper, 7-7/8 x 5-7/16 inches. India, Punjab Hills, Basohli Style, ca.1700. Edward L. Whittemore Fund. 66.27

153 *Shakyamuni.* Gilt bronze, H. 17-3/8 inches. China, Yüan Dynasty, 14th century. Purchase from the J. H. Wade Fund. 66.116

154 *Shino ware Dish.* Nezumé (mouse gray) type, stoneware, 7-7/8 x 9-3/16 inches. Japan, Momoyama Period, 1573–1615. John L. Severance Fund. 66.24

155 *Sita in the Garden of Lanka with Ravana and His Demons,* The Siege of Lanka sequence from *The Ramayana.* Gold and color on paper, 22-3/4 x 33-1/4 inches. India, Rajputana, Punjab Hills, Guler, ca.1720.
Collections: A. K. Coomaraswamy; Raja Raghunath Singh of Guler.
Exhibited: New York, Asia House Gallery, 1960: Rajput Painting.
Published: Sherman E. Lee, *Rajput Painting* (New York: Asia House, 1960), p. 77.
Gift of George P. Bickford. 66.143

156 *Standing Buddha.* Brass, H. 38-5/8 inches. North India or Kashmir, early 8th century A.D. John L. Severance Fund. 66.30

157 *Standing Figure of a Beauty: Kakiemon Type.* Porcelain decorated in over-glaze colored enamels, H. 14-15/16 inches. Japan, Edo Period, late 17th century. John L. Severance Fund. 64.366

158 *Surya, the Sun God.* Brass, H. 19-13/16 inches. Kashmir, early 8th century. Gift of Katharine Holden Thayer. 65.557

159 *Teapot with Cover: Arita ware.* Porcelain with colored enamel decoration, H. 6-3/8 inches. Japan, Edo Period, 1615–1868. The Norweb Collection. 66.146,a